MAKE-IT MODELS

MAKE A
CASTLE

Anna Claybourne

CRABTREE
PUBLISHING COMPANY
WWW.CRABTREEBOOKS.COM

CRABTREE
PUBLISHING COMPANY
WWW.CRABTREEBOOKS.COM

Published in Canada
Crabtree Publishing
616 Welland Avenue
St. Catharines, ON
L2M 5V6

Published in the United States
Crabtree Publishing
PMB 59051
350 Fifth Ave, 59th Floor
New York, NY 10118

Published in 2020 by Crabtree Publishing Company

First published in Great Britain in 2019 by Wayland
Copyright © Hodder and Stoughton, 2019

Author: Anna Claybourne

Editorial director: Kathy Middleton

Editors: Elise Short, Elizabeth DiEmanuele

Proofreader: Wendy Scavuzzo

Design and illustration: Collaborate

Production coordinator and prepress: Ken Wright

Print coordinator: Katherine Berti

Printed in the U.S.A./122019/CG20191101

The website addresses (URLs) included in this book were valid at the time of going to press. However, it is possible that contents or addresses may have changed since the publication of this book. No responsibility for any such changes can be accepted by either the author or the Publisher.

Note: In preparation of this book, all due care has been exercised with regard to the instructions, activities, and techniques depicted. The publishers regret that they can accept no liability for any loss or injury sustained. Always get adult supervision and follow manufacturers' advice when using electric and battery-powered appliances.

Library and Archives Canada Cataloguing in Publication

Title: Make a castle / Anna Claybourne.
Other titles: Castle
Names: Claybourne, Anna, author.
Description: Series statement: Make-it models |
  Previously published under title: Castle.
  London: Wayland, 2019. | Includes index.
Identifiers: Canadiana (print) 20190200359 |
  Canadiana (ebook) 20190200367 |
  ISBN 9780778773542 (hardcover) |
  ISBN 9780778773672 (softcover) |
  ISBN 9781427124937 (HTML)
Subjects: LCSH: Castles—Models—Juvenile literature. |
  LCSH: Models and modelmaking—Juvenile literature.
Classification: LCC NA7710 .C53 2020 |
  DDC j728.8/10228—dc23

Library of Congress Cataloging-in-Publication Data

Names: Claybourne, Anna, author.
Title: Make a Castle / Anna Claybourne.
Description: New York, New York : Crabtree Publishing
  Company, [2019] | Series: Make-it models | "First published in
  Great Britain in 2019 by Wayland"--Colophon.
Identifiers: LCCN 2019043477 (print) |
  LCCN 2019043478 (ebook) |
  ISBN 9780778773542 (hardcover) |
  ISBN 9780778773672 (paperback) |
  ISBN 9781427124937 (ebook)
Subjects: LCSH: Castles--Models--Juvenile literature. |
  Architectural models--Juvenile literature. |
  Handicraft--Juvenile literature.
Classification: LCC NA7710 .C55 2019 (print) |
  LCC NA7710 (ebook) | DDC 720.22--dc23
LC record available at https://lccn.loc.gov/2019043477
LC ebook record available at https://lccn.loc.gov/2019043478

CONTENTS

Holding the Fort 4
Castle Walls and Battlements 6
Towers and Turrets 8
The Grand Gatehouse 10
Door and Portcullis 12
Raise the Drawbridge! 14
The Great Hall 16
The Bedchamber 18
The Secret Room 20
The Tilt Yard 22
Mangonel Attack! 24
The Grounds and Moat 26
And Here Is Your Finished Castle! 28
Glossary 30
Further Information 31
Index 32

HOLDING THE FORT

Since ancient times, people have built castles and forts: big stone buildings designed to guard the land around them and keep enemies out. They were often homes, too, for kings, queens, lords, ladies, and **knights**.

If you love castles, knights, and fairytales, this book is for you. It shows you how to build your own castle, complete with a working door, **drawbridge**, **moat**, **turrets**, and waving flags. There is also a **tilt yard** for **jousting** knights and a **mangonel** for battles—all made from cardboard boxes, craft materials, and other everyday items.

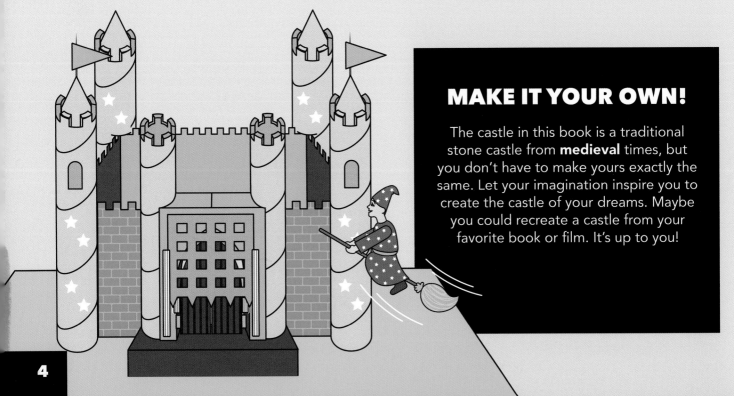

MAKE IT YOUR OWN!

The castle in this book is a traditional stone castle from **medieval** times, but you don't have to make yours exactly the same. Let your imagination inspire you to create the castle of your dreams. Maybe you could recreate a castle from your favorite book or film. It's up to you!

MAKE-IT MATERIALS

The projects in this book use items you can find at home, such as reusable containers, packaging, and basic arts and crafts equipment. If you don't have what you need, you can usually get it at a craft store, grocery store, or by ordering online. Go to page 31 for a list of useful sources.

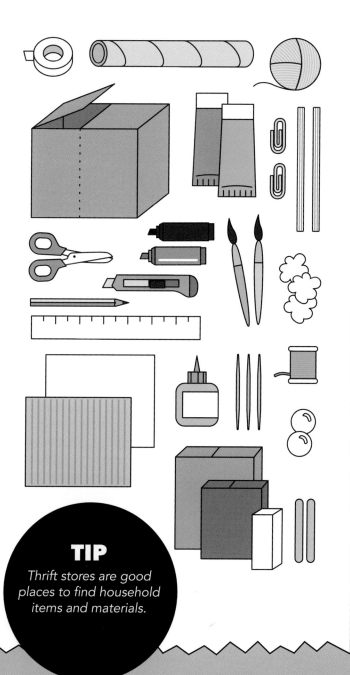

TIP
Thrift stores are good places to find household items and materials.

SAFETY ALERT!

For some of the projects, you will need to use sharp tools, such as a craft knife or a bradawl (a pointed tool for making holes). You might also want to use an electric appliance, such as a hot **glue gun**.

For anything involving sharp objects, heat, or electricity, always ask an adult to help and supervise. Make sure you keep items like these in a safe place.

CAN I USE THIS?

Before getting started, make sure your containers and household items are clean and ready to use. Also check for permission to use them. Let the castle-making begin!

CASTLE WALLS AND BATTLEMENTS

Start by making the basic structure of your castle from a cardboard box. This will include the castle walls and **battlements**, the upper part of a castle or fort. The box can be any size, but a medium-sized box is best.

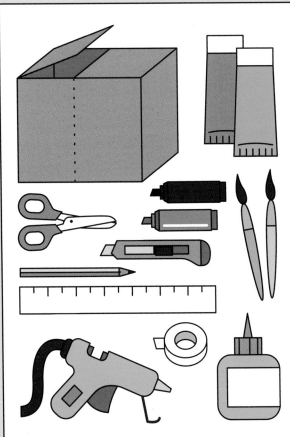

WHAT YOU NEED

- A corrugated cardboard box
- Scissors and a craft knife
- A ruler
- A pencil
- Superglue or a glue gun
- Paints and paintbrushes
- Felt-tip pens or markers
- Clear tape

1 Make sure the base of your box is taped together. With a ruler and pencil, draw a line around the box to make a wall about 8–12 inches (20–30 cm) high. Cut along the line to remove the top of the box. Keep the spare cardboard!

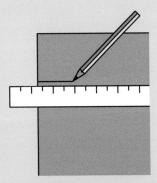

2 Draw battlements along the tops of the castle walls, making them about 1 inch (2.5 cm) wide. Carefully cut out the battlements.

3 Using the spare cardboard, cut four long strips, each about 1 inch (2.5 cm) wide. Make two the same length as the box, and two the same width as the box.

4 Use a ruler and pencil to draw a line lengthwise down the middle of each strip, pressing hard to bend the cardboard. Fold the strips along the lines.

5 Arrange the strips inside the castle just below the battlements, making them overlap at the corners. Glue them in place. These are the walkways that allow guards to stand on the battlements.

6 Cut another long strip of cardboard just about 1 inch (2 cm) wide, and make a fold every 0.5 inches (1 cm), folding first one way, then the other to make steps. Fold small strips of cardboard in half to make tabs. These should be about 0.5 inches (1 cm) wide and just about 1 inch (2 cm) long. Use these to glue the steps onto the inside of one wall, leading up to the walkway.

7 To decorate your castle, paint the walls all over. When it's dry, draw stones.

THE HISTORY PART!

Long ago, kings, queens, lords, ladies, and knights had castles to live in and to control the surrounding area. During wars and battles, people stayed in castles to be safe, so they had to be strong and well defended.

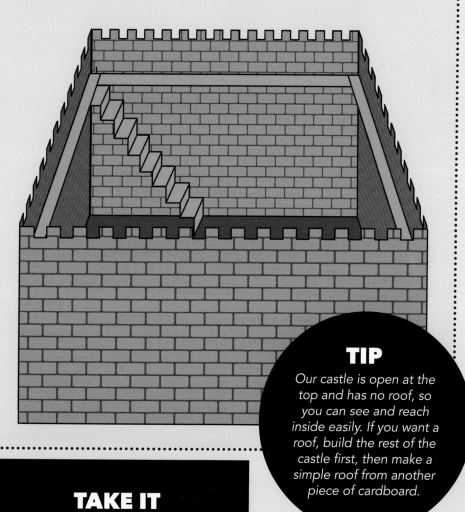

TIP

Our castle is open at the top and has no roof, so you can see and reach inside easily. If you want a roof, build the rest of the castle first, then make a simple roof from another piece of cardboard.

TAKE IT FURTHER

For a bigger, more complicated castle, you can prepare more boxes in the same way and glue them to the first one.

TOWERS AND TURRETS

Your castle doesn't look like a castle yet, because it needs towers and turrets. (A turret is a small tower at the corner of a building or wall, or on top of a larger tower.) They're easy to make from cardboard tubes.

WHAT YOU NEED

- Four strong, wide cardboard tubes, such as poster tubes or potato chip tubes
- A plastic lid that is larger in diameter than the cardboard tubes
- Scissors and a craft knife
- A pencil and a ruler
- Card stock
- Superglue or a glue gun
- Clear tape
- Toothpicks
- Paper
- Felt-tip pens or markers
- Paints and paintbrushes

Empty paper towel tubes will work too, but they will make narrower towers, and won't be quite as strong.

1 Cut your tubes to a good height for your towers, about 4 inches (10 cm) taller than your castle walls. If you're using long poster tubes, you may be able to cut two or more castle towers from each one.

2 Hold one tube against your castle walls and draw on the height of the wall all around your tube. Turn the tube upside down and mark its base into quarters. Pick two lines next to each other and draw lines from those marks up the sides of the tube, to the line marking the height of your castle walls.

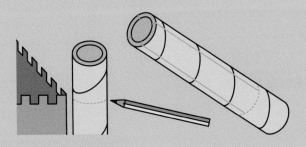

3 On a piece of card stock, draw four circles by tracing around the end of a tower. Draw a 0.5-inch (1 cm) border around each circle. Cut them out. Cut slits into the edges to make tabs, and fold them down.

4 Carefully cut out this shape with scissors or a craft knife. Repeat steps 2 and 4 for the other tubes. Check to see how the towers fit the corners of the castle.

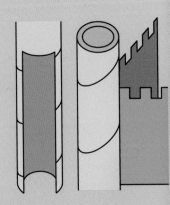

5 Mark battlements around the tops of the tubes and cut them out. You can also draw windows or **arrow slits** on the towers and cut them out, too. Below the battlements, glue the circles inside the tops of the towers.

6 Using the plastic lid, draw two bigger circles on card stock. Draw a 0.5-inch (1 cm) border around both circles and cut them out. Cut each circle in half. Cut into the curved edges to make tabs. Curve each piece around to make a pointed turret roof that will fit inside the towers. Tape each roof together.

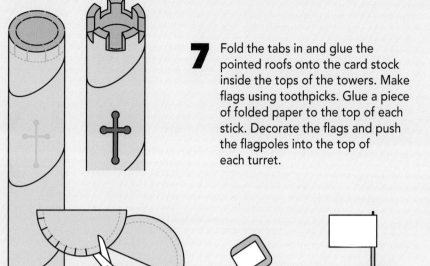

7 Fold the tabs in and glue the pointed roofs onto the card stock inside the tops of the towers. Make flags using toothpicks. Glue a piece of folded paper to the top of each stick. Decorate the flags and push the flagpoles into the top of each turret.

8 If you like, paint or decorate the towers. When they are dry, attach the towers to the corners of the castle. Use glue to hold them in place.

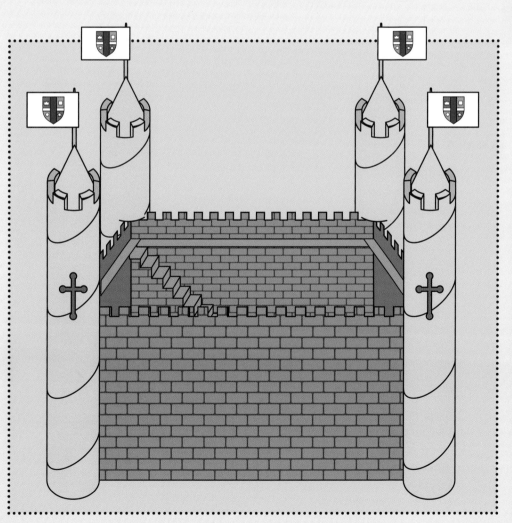

THE HISTORY PART!

Wealthy families, knights, or rulers often had their own **coats of arms**: a shield-shaped symbol made up of colors and pictures. You could design a coat of arms for your flags.

THE GRAND GATEHOUSE

At the front of every good castle is the **gatehouse**—a grand entrance with its own mini turrets.

WHAT YOU NEED

- Two flat cardboard boxes, one larger, one smaller
- Two cardboard tubes (empty paper towel tubes are perfect)
- Scissors and a craft knife
- A pencil and a ruler
- Card stock
- Superglue or a glue gun
- Wooden skewers or cocktail sticks
- Paper
- Felt-tip pens or markers
- Paints and paintbrushes

The larger box should be thinner than your cardboard tubes, but taller than the height of the castle walls. Chocolate boxes are a good option. The smaller box should be a similar width to the larger box, but shorter and thinner.

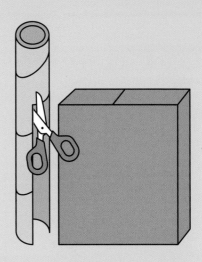

1 Hold the side of the larger box against one of the cardboard tubes. Trace around it onto the tube. Cut out the shape so that the tube can slot into the side of the box. Do the same with the other tube.

2 Draw small battlements around the tops of the two tubes and cut them out. You can also make turret roofs and flags, as shown on pages 8–9, or you can just leave them as they are.

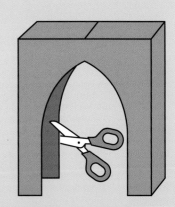

3 Draw an arched or rounded doorway on the front and center of the larger box. Cut out the doorway from both the front and the back of the box.

4 Cut a long strip of card stock (the length of the outline of the archway). It should be wide enough to fit in the gap between the front and back of the archway with an extra 0.5 inches (1 cm) along each side. Cut slits into the sides to make tabs. Carefully glue this strip along the inside edge of the doorway.

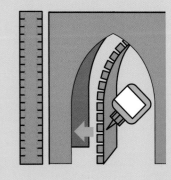

5 Glue the towers into place on the sides of the box. Then take the smaller box and stand the gatehouse on top of it. Glue the gatehouse together.

6 Once the glue is dry, stand the gatehouse up against the front of the castle. Draw lines on the castle walls about 0.5 inches (1 cm) in from each edge of the gatehouse towers. Carefully cut out and remove the section from the front of the castle between the two marks.

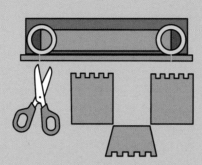

7 Cut slits in the outside edges of the gatehouse, through the tubes and the smaller box, so that you can slot it into the castle walls.

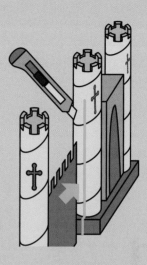

8 If needed, trim a small amount off of the ends of the walkway to get a good fit. Once you're happy with the position of the gatehouse, glue it into place.

Finally, if you like, you can paint the gatehouse and draw patterns to look like stonework.

DOOR AND PORTCULLIS

A castle is not complete without a sturdy wooden door and an iron portcullis. A portcullis is a strong metal gate that can be lowered down over a doorway to protect against invaders.

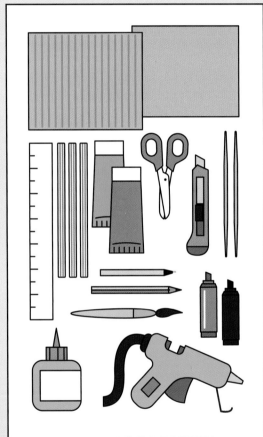

WHAT YOU NEED

- Thick corrugated cardboard
- Card stock
- Scissors and a craft knife
- A pencil and a ruler
- Superglue or a glue gun
- Wooden skewers
- Three straws
- Paints and paintbrushes
- Felt-tip pens or markers
- Silver paint or pen

1 On the cardboard, draw a door shape that will fit loosely inside the archway of your gatehouse. Cut it out. Draw around it to make a matching door.

2 Cut four small pieces of card stock, about 0.5 inches (1 cm) wide by a bit more than 1 inch (2.5 cm) long. Fold them in half. Glue two on each side of one of the door shapes. Make sure the folded edges stick out a little.

3 Glue the second door shape on top of the first, so that the tabs are sandwiched in between them and the folds stick out at the sides to make hinges. If you like, you can paint or color the door.

4 Measure the length between the two hinges on each side of the door. Cut two pieces of straw just slightly shorter than this length.

5 Now measure the length between the upper and lower edges of the hinges. Cut two pieces of wooden skewer slightly longer than this length.

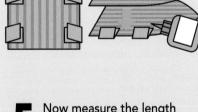

6 Fit the straws in the gaps between the hinges. Push the skewers through the hinges and through the straws in between them. The hinges should hold the skewers tightly, but if they don't, add a bit of glue. (DON'T get glue on the straw!)

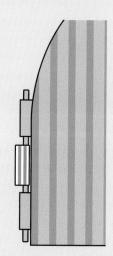

7 Carefully cut the door in half to make two doors. Check that they fit inside the gatehouse. If they don't, trim a little off the middle edge of each door.

8 Use glue to attach the straws to the insides of the gatehouse doorway, so the doors meet in the middle. When the glue is dry, you should be able to open and close the doors.

PORTCULLIS

1 Cut along one side of the two remaining straws. Position and glue the two straws onto the sides of the gatehouse, next to the towers, with the cut sides facing each other.

2 Measure the width between the outer edges of the straws. On card stock, draw a portcullis the same width across. Cut it out and color or paint it silver (or gray if you don't have silver). When it's dry, slide it between the straws, so it can slide up and down.

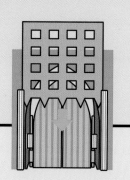

TIP

If you have silver-colored card stock, it will make a great portcullis. You can sometimes find it in packaging or in a craft store.

RAISE THE DRAWBRIDGE!

For extra security, many castles had a moat (body of water) with a drawbridge across it. The drawbridge could be raised so that enemies couldn't get across the water.

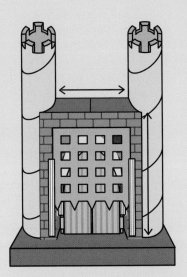

1 Measure the width between the gatehouse towers and the height of the middle of the gatehouse. On cardboard, draw a rectangle with this width and height. Cut it out.

2 Use a bradawl or needle to make four small holes in the corners of the rectangle. If you like, you can paint or color it to look like wooden planks.

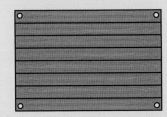

WHAT YOU NEED

- Cardboard
- A non-bendy straw
- Scissors and a craft knife
- A pencil and a ruler
- Superglue or a glue gun
- Thick string
- A bradawl or a sewing needle
- Paints and paintbrushes
- Felt-tip pens or markers
- Two metal paper clips

A straw should work for this, but if it's not long enough, try using a long chopstick or wooden skewer instead.

3 Take the two paper clips, unfold them and bend them into U-shapes with one longer side. Loop them into the holes in one end of the drawbridge. Push the ends into the base of the gatehouse, in between the towers. (If it's hard to get them in, make small holes first.)

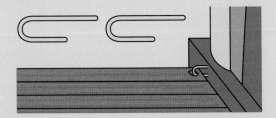

4 Use a bit of glue to stick the paper clips in place, with the loops sticking out a little way so that the drawbridge can move up and down.

5 Cut two pieces of string, each about 20 inches (50 cm) long. Tie the ends of the strings into the two holes at the other end of the drawbridge.

6 Mark dots on the sides of both of the gatehouse towers, using a ruler to make sure they are all at the same level. Use a sharp pencil to make holes just big enough for the straw to fit through.

7 Push the straw through all the holes. Take the loose ends of the two strings and tie them around the middle of the straw. Glue them down, so the string cannot slip around the straw.

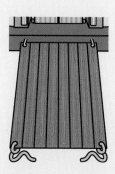

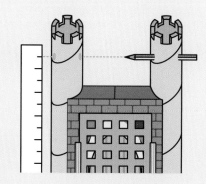

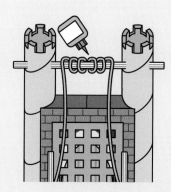

8 When the glue is dry, turn the straw round and round so the string winds around it, pulling the drawbridge up. To lower the drawbridge, turn the straw the other way!

THE HISTORY PART!

Invading a castle with a raised drawbridge was tough. Guards fired arrows at attackers from the top of the gatehouse. The raised drawbridge and the portcullis protected the doorway, but if anyone did get in, the guards dropped rocks, hot oil, or boiling water on them. Ouch!

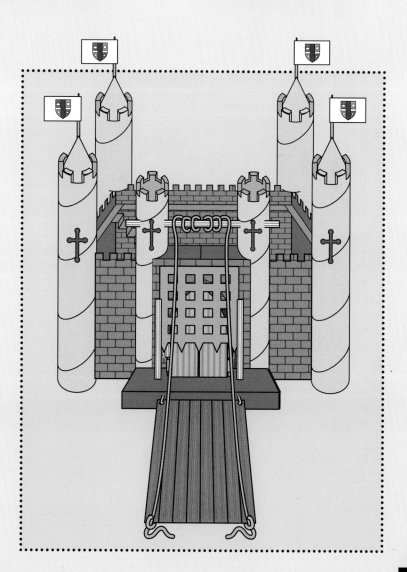

THE GREAT HALL

The great hall is the biggest room in the castle, where feasts and dances are held. It has dining tables and benches, lit by candlelight.

1 Measure the inside of the castle from front to back and one-third of the distance across it. Mark these measurements underneath the shoebox. Cut this shape out and fit it inside the castle to make a room on one side.

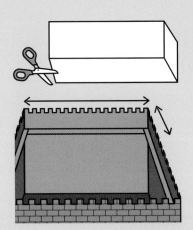

2 The remaining space is the great hall. Measure its length and width, and cut out a piece of paper the right size to fit inside. Paint or draw floorboards on the paper. When it's dry, glue it to the floor of the main hall.

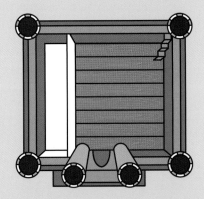

3 If you like, you can decorate the walls inside the hall with medieval **tapestry** wall hangings. Draw them on pieces of paper and color them in, then glue them to the walls.

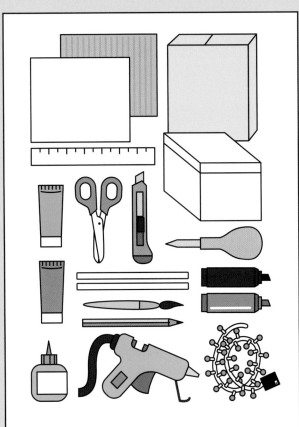

WHAT YOU NEED

- A strong cardboard box, such as a shoebox
- Paper
- Scissors and a craft knife
- A pencil and a ruler
- Paints and paintbrushes
- Felt-tip pens or markers
- Cardboard
- Strong glue or a glue gun
- A flat wide cardboard box
- Clear tape
- A bradawl or a sewing needle
- Small battery-powered string lights (optional)
- White straws (optional)

4 To make a dining table, cut a long rectangle from cardboard, a thinner strip of cardboard the same length, and two small shapes. Fold the small shapes in half and glue them to the table to make legs. Cut slits in the legs. Fit the card stock strip into them.

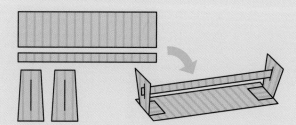

5 You can make benches the same way. Just make them lower and thinner. Make two benches for each table and arrange them around the hall.

6 To make a row of candles, cut the end off the wide flat box to make a long shallow tray shape. Use the bradawl to make a row of holes along one side.

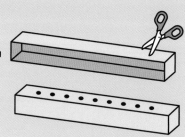

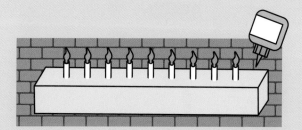

7 If you have a set of string lights, make a hole in the castle's back wall and thread the string lights through it. Leave the battery hidden behind the castle. Poke a light through each hole in the tray, so it sticks up like a candle. Tape down the wire inside the tray.

8 Glue the tray to the wall over the hole you made, with the lights sticking up, and switch them on. Or, if you don't have string lights, stick model candles along the tray, made of short pieces of a white straw with a colored paper flame on top.

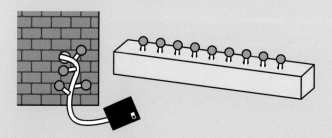

TAKE IT FURTHER

What else could you add? Try designing and making a fireplace, a throne, or even tiny plates, **goblets**, and food.

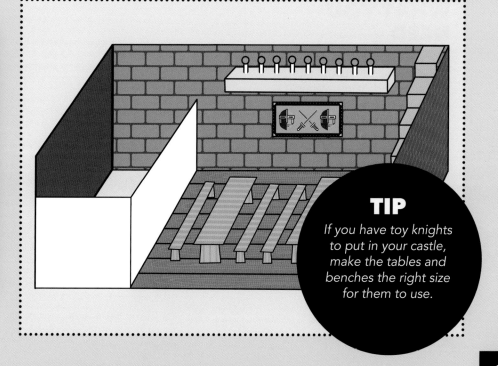

TIP

If you have toy knights to put in your castle, make the tables and benches the right size for them to use.

THE BEDCHAMBER

The lord or lady of a castle had their own fancy bedroom, known as a bedchamber, complete with a four-poster bed and a close stool. What was a close stool? A type of toilet that looked like a chair!

WHAT YOU NEED

- Paper and card stock
- Scissors and a craft knife
- Paints and paintbrushes
- White glue
- Felt-tip pens or markers
- Small cardboard boxes, such as medicine or makeup boxes
- A sharp pencil
- Non-bendy straws
- Superglue or a glue gun
- White tissues
- Cotton balls
- Scraps of fabric

1 Measure the size of the smaller room you have made in your castle. This is the bedchamber. Cut a piece of paper to fit. Decorate it to look like floorboards or floor tiles and glue it to the floor. Cut a doorway into the bedchamber wall.

2 Make a rug for the room by drawing a rug pattern onto a piece of card stock.

3 For the bed, take a small box. Draw a line all around it, about 1 inch (2.5 cm) from the edge. Mark another line 0.5 inches (1 cm) from the other edge. Cut along the lines to make two tray-shaped parts.

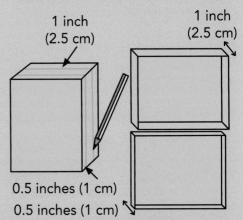

1 inch (2.5 cm)

1 inch (2.5 cm)

0.5 inches (1 cm)

0.5 inches (1 cm)

4 Paint or color the outsides of the two parts to look like wood, using markers or paint mixed with an equal amount of white glue.

5 Use a sharp pencil to make four holes in the corners of the deeper tray. Cut four pieces of straw about 2–2.5 inches (5–6 cm) long and color them brown. Stick them into the four holes, and glue them in place underneath. Fit the shallower tray on top of the straws and glue it in place to make the canopy.

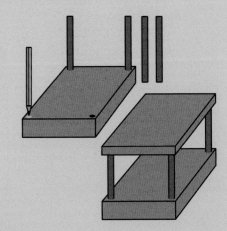

6 To make a pillow, fold a tissue around some cotton balls and glue it down. Use pieces of fabric to make bedcovers.

7 For the close stool, cut a piece off of the end of a small, long box, such as a lipstick box. Cut a round hole in the top. Cut the flap from the other end of the box and glue it to the side of the stool to make a seat cover.

8 Cut a longer rectangle of card stock and stick it to the back of the stool, over where the flap is stuck on. Finally, paint or decorate the close stool.

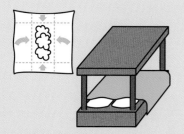
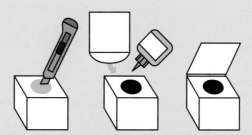

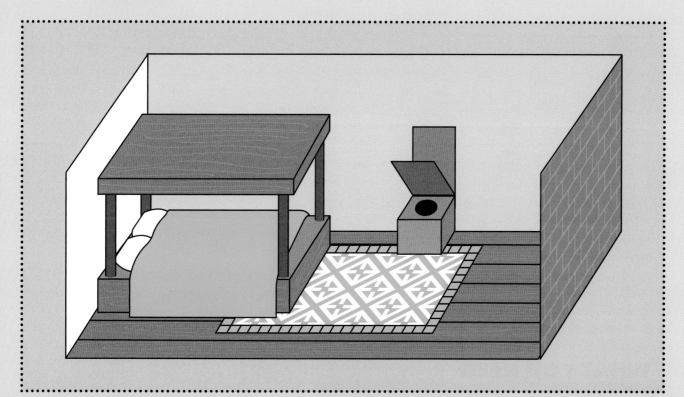

THE HISTORY PART!

In medieval times, castles didn't have toilets that could be flushed. A bowl inside the close-stool collected the waste, and an unlucky servant would have to empty it!

TAKE IT FURTHER

What else could you design and make for the bedchamber? What about **wood paneling** for the walls, or a portrait painting? The lord or lady might also like a candlestick, a pet dog, or a tiny book to read.

THE SECRET ROOM

If someone is on the run and lying low in the castle, keep them well hidden in a secret room with a hidden revolving door.

WHAT YOU NEED

- Cardboard
- Paper
- Scissors and a craft knife
- Felt-tip pens or markers
- Superglue or a glue gun
- A wooden skewer
- Small cardboard boxes
- White tissues
- Cotton balls
- Scraps of fabric

1 Measure the width and height of your bedchamber. Cut a piece of cardboard the same size to make a wall. Make sure the lines in the cardboard run up and down, so that when you look at the top of the wall, you can see a row of little holes.

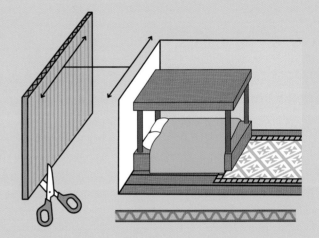

2 Use felt-tip pens or markers to draw shelves full of books on the wall.

3 Draw a small door shape on the wall with the bottom a little above the floor. Use a ruler to make sure it is a perfect rectangle. Carefully cut out the door, leaving a neat hole in the wall.

4 On the back of the door, draw the same pattern of books as on the front.

5 Fit the door into the hole in the wall. Push the pointy end of the skewer up through the cardboard in the base of the wall, and up through the middle of the door. At the top of the door, push it through into the wall.

6 Cut off the skewer so that it is level with the bottom of the wall. You should now be able to swivel the door around to open and close it. When it's closed, it will blend in with the bookshelves.

7 Fit the wall into one end of the bedchamber, leaving a small space behind it. Use some glue to hold it in place. If you like, you can also make a small bed, close stool (see pages 18–19), and other furniture and objects for the secret room.

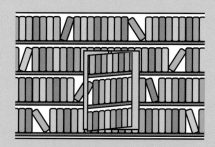

THE HISTORY PART!

In 1745, Alexander Irvine, the Laird (or Lord) of Drum Castle in Scotland, fought for the Scottish **Jacobites** against the English in the famous Battle of Culloden. The Jacobites lost and Alexander fled for his life. His sister Mary kept him hidden in a secret room at Drum Castle for three years to avoid capture by the English.

THE TILT YARD

To practice their skills and provide entertainment, medieval knights took part in jousting contests. Two knights charged toward each other and each tried to knock the other off his horse, using a long **lance**. This took place on a special jousting ground called a tilt yard.

1 Using a ruler and pencil, draw a rectangle about 5 inches (12 cm) wide and 18 inches (45 cm) long on the cardboard. Cut it out. Cut a long strip of cardboard, the same length as your rectangle and about 0.5 inches (1 cm) wide.

2 Cut about 40 1–1.5-inch (2.5–3 cm) long pieces of skewer or toothpick. Draw a line down the middle of the large cardboard rectangle. Use a skewer or toothpick to make a row of holes along the line about 0.5 inches (1 cm) apart.

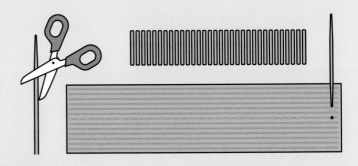

3 Stick the pieces of skewer or toothpick into the holes and secure them with glue. Take the long strip of cardboard and fit it on top of the row of sticks, pushing them in between the layers of cardboard. Add some glue if needed.

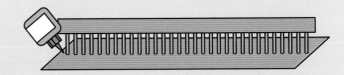

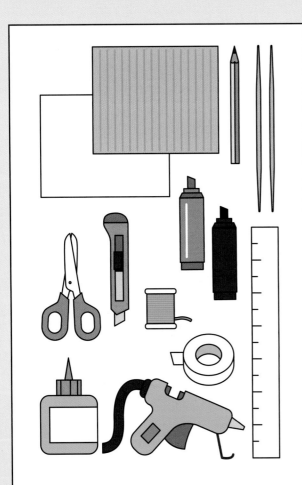

WHAT YOU NEED

- Strong cardboard
- A ruler and a pencil
- Wooden skewers or toothpicks
- Superglue or a glue gun
- Clear tape
- Card stock
- Scissors and a craft knife
- Felt-tip pens or markers
- Strong sewing thread

4 On the card stock, draw two knights on horseback about 2.5 inches (6 cm) long. You could copy or trace a picture from a book or from the Internet, or copy the knight on this page. Carefully cut the knights out and color them in with felt-tip pens or markers.

5 Cut two door-shaped pieces of corrugated cardboard about 1 inch (2 cm) wide and 2.5 inches (6 cm) long. Cut two pieces of skewer or toothpick about 2 inches (5 cm) long. Stick the pointed ends at a right angle into the middle of the pieces of cardboard.

6 Use glue or clear tape to attach the knights to the sticks. Take two longer pieces of skewer and attach them to the knights to act as lances.

7 Use a skewer or toothpick to make a small hole in the front of each door-shaped piece of card stock. Tie a piece of thread about 19.5 inches (50 cm) long into each one.

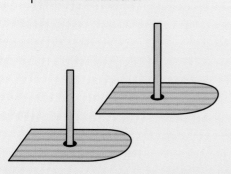

8 You can now line up the knights on each side of the tilt yard, and pull the strings to make them charge toward each other.

TIP

If the knights don't stand up easily, they may need wider bases.

TAKE IT FURTHER

Can you build stands for the audience to sit on to watch the jousting?

TIP

Give the knights different colored horse blankets and helmet **plumes**, *so that the audience can tell them apart!*

MANGONEL ATTACK!

If enemies decide to **besiege** your castle, they'll probably bring their mangonel. This is a giant catapult used to shoot rocks at castles to smash down their walls. Yikes!

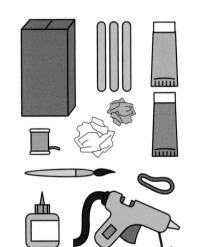

WHAT YOU NEED

- 30 craft sticks
- Superglue or a glue gun
- Thin string or strong sewing thread
- A strong rubber band
- A small or narrow cardboard box
- Newspaper or scrap paper
- Paint and paintbrushes (optional)

If your craft sticks and string are a natural color, you don't need to paint them. They'll look realistic as they are.

1 Glue two craft sticks together so that they overlap in the middle. Repeat with another two sticks. The mangonel has to be very strong, so you also need to wrap string or thread around the joins several times and tightly tie it together.

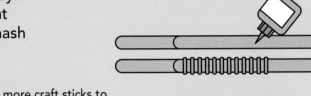

2 Glue two more craft sticks to each piece to make triangle shapes. They should overlap slightly at the top. Before joining the last corner, thread one strong rubber band onto both triangles. When the glue is dry, use more string or thread to wrap around and strengthen the joins.

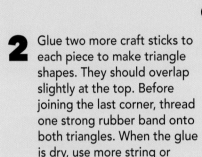

3 Glue about 20 craft sticks together in a block to make a strong base for the mangonel. Line up the triangle-shaped pieces on each side of the base, and glue them. Strengthen the structure by wrapping and tying more string or thread around it.

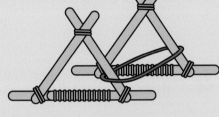

4 Cut or break a craft stick to fit across the top of the two triangles. Use string to tie both ends on tightly. At this point, if you like, you can paint the mangonel and leave it to dry.

5 Twist the middle of the rubber band around a few times, then push a craft stick into the middle of it.

6 Position the craft stick so that one end of it is held by the rubber band, and the rest reaches through the mangonel frame, between the triangles. The rubber band should make it spring up against the top bar. (If it doesn't, try twisting the rubber band the other way.)

7 Cut a tray shape from the end of your small cardboard box and glue it to the top of the long end of the stick. You can now place a missile in the tray, pull the stick down, and release it to fire.

8 To make realistic rocks, scrunch up balls of newspaper or scrap paper, make them an uneven shape, and paint them gray. You can use some glue to make sure the paper stays scrunched up.

THE HISTORY PART!

In addition to rocks, attackers sometimes used a mangonel to fling dead animals over the walls to spread disease, or bundles of burning rags to try to start a fire.

THE GROUNDS AND MOAT

Most castles have large enclosed grounds around them, sometimes with a moat and more buildings, too. Your tilt yard can go here, as well.

1 Cut the cardboard into the shape you want. It could be a square, oval, hexagon, or whatever you like, but make sure you keep it as large as possible. Pick up your castle and position it in the middle.

WHAT YOU NEED

- A very large piece of cardboard
- Thick card stock
- Scissors and a craft knife
- Felt-tip pens or markers
- Paints and paintbrushes
- Superglue or a glue gun
- Clear plastic food bags
- Smaller cardboard boxes and tubes
- Green paper or white glitter
- Small dry twigs with several branches
- Modeling clay
- Felt or fabric (optional)
- Sand and small pebbles (optional)

You can get a really big piece of cardboard from the box of a large appliance, such as a washing machine. If you can't find one, tape several smaller pieces of cardboard together.

2 Use strips of thick cardboard to make a low outer wall around the grounds. These should be about 3–4 inches (7–10 cm) wide. Fold over about 0.5 inches (1 cm) at the base of each piece of wall to glue them to the edge of the grounds. Leave an open gateway facing the front door of the castle.

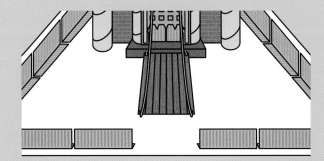

3 Use a marker or felt-tip pen to draw a moat around the castle, making sure it is narrow enough for the drawbridge to cross it. Add a path from the gateway up to the drawbridge. You could also use small narrow cardboard boxes or tubes to make gateposts.

4 Paint the pathway a stone color and the rest of the grounds a grassy green. If you have green felt or fabric, you could use that to make the grass instead. You could also cover the pathway with glue, sprinkle it with sand, and arrange pebbles along the sides.

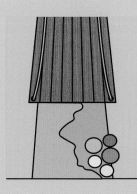

5 Paint the moat a watery blue or blue-green color. When the paint is dry, cover it with a layer of clear plastic cut from food bags. You can also add pebbles along the edges of the moat.

6 Make trees using small branching twigs stuck into pieces of brown modeling clay to help them stand up. Make little leaves from paper and glue them on. For a wintery scene, put some glue along the tops of the branches and sprinkle them with white glitter.

7 A **dovecot** is a nesting house for pigeons, which were then put into pies! Make one using a round box or cardboard tube. Make a flat roof from a circle of card stock, with a hole in the middle so the pigeons can fly in and out. Decorate it to look as though it's made of stone and add a little door.

TAKE IT FURTHER

If you want to add even more things to your castle, what about a stable for the knights' horses, a walled rose garden, or strings of tiny paper buntings?

TIP

Keep your castle in a safe place and don't leave it where anyone could trip over it!

AND HERE IS YOUR FINISHED CASTLE!

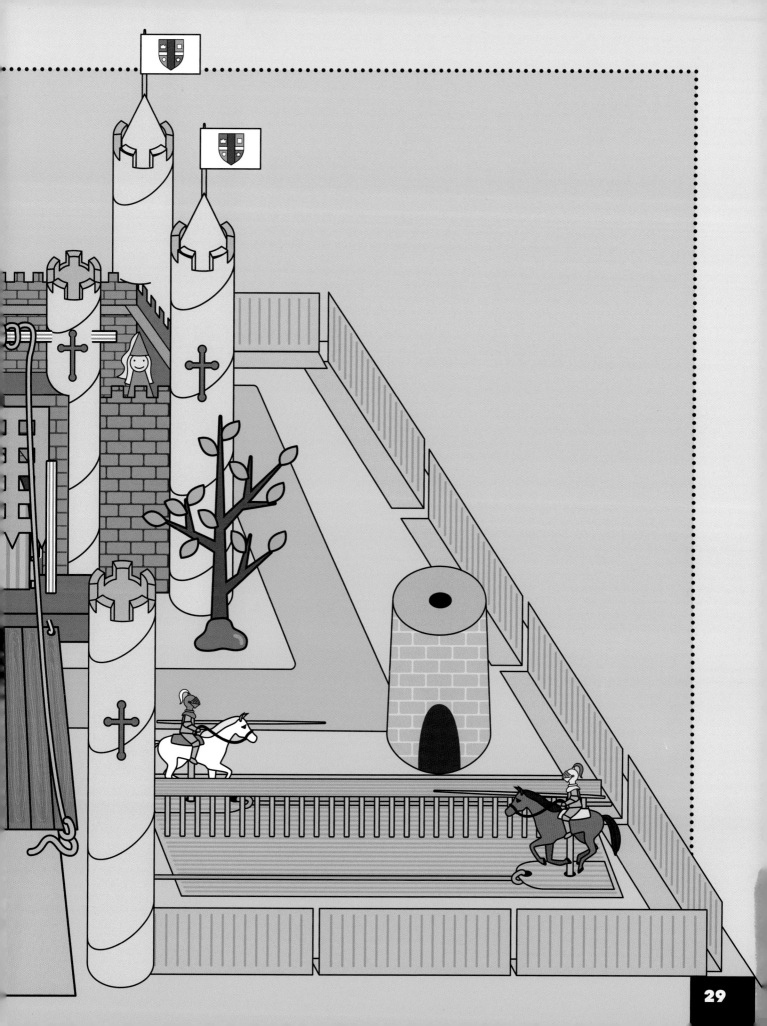

GLOSSARY

arrow slits Tall, narrow castle windows that arrows can be fired from

battlements Walls around the top of a castle with regular spaces in them

besiege To surround and attack a castle

coats of arms Shield-shaped pictures or designs used to represent a family, town, or organization

dovecot A building for pigeons to shelter and nest in

drawbridge A bridge over a castle moat, which can be raised to prevent enemies from crossing the moat

gatehouse A strong building surrounding the entrance to a castle

glue gun An electric tool that heats up and applies strong glue

goblets Old-fashioned, bowl-shaped drinking cups with stems

Jacobites Supporters of the Stuart royal family of King James II of England, who wanted the Stuarts to rule England and Scotland

jousting A sport in which two knights used lances to try to knock each other off their horses

knights Armed soldiers who rode horses and served a lord or king

lance A long wooden spear with a pointed steel tip

mangonel A machine used to fire rocks and other large missiles at a castle

medieval Dating from the Middle Ages in Europe, the period from around 500 to 1500 CE

moat A deep, wide, water-filled ditch surrounding a castle to keep enemies out

plumes Bunch of long feathers worn on top of a helmet

tapestry A thick cloth with threads sewn or woven into it to make patterns or pictures

tilt yard An area for holding jousting contests

turrets Small towers at the corners of a building or wall, or on top of a larger tower

wood paneling Thin sheets of wood used to cover a wall

FURTHER INFORMATION

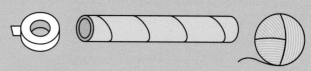

WHERE TO GET MATERIALS

Everyday items
You'll probably have some everyday items and craft materials at home already, such as foil, pens, tissues, string, paper, card stock, clear tape, glue, and scissors.

Recycling
Old packaging that's going to be thrown away or recycled is a great source of making materials, such as cardboard boxes, yogurt containers, ice cream tubs, cardboard tubes, magazines, old wrapping paper, and newspaper.

Grocery stores
Great for basic items you might not have at home, such as paper cups, cotton balls, a sewing kit, paper straws, toothpicks, and battery-powered string lights.

Outdoors
Collect items such as leaves, twigs, acorns, and shells for free!

Specialty stores
Hobby and craft stores, art stores, garden centers, and DIY stores could be useful for things like a craft knife, a glue gun, modeling clay, fabric, sand, and pebbles. If you don't have the store you need near you, ask an adult to help you look online.

Thrift stores
It's always a good idea to check thrift stores when you can, as they often have all kinds of handy household items and craft materials at very low prices.

BOOKS

Biesty, Stephen. *Stephen Biesty's Cross-Sections: Castle*. DK Children, 2019.

Bow, James. *Your Guide to Castles and Medieval Warfare*. Crabtree Publishing, 2017.

Boyer, Crispin. *Everything Castles*. National Geographic, 2011.

Deary, Terry. *Dark Knights and Dingy Castles*. Scholastic, 2017.

WEBSITES

Parents.com Arts & Crafts
https://www.parents.com/fun/arts-crafts/?page=1
Check out maker projects, instructions, and videos.

PBS Design Squad
https://pbskids.org/designsquad/
Visit this site for lots of fun designing and building challenges..

Kiwico DIY page
https://www.kiwico.com/diy/
A website of fun and easy maker ideas.

INDEX

B
battlements 6, 7, 8, 9, 10, 28, 29
battles 4, 7, 21
bed 18, 19, 21

C
close stool 18, 19, 21
coat of arms 9, 29

D
dances 16
door 4, 12–13, 20, 21, 26
doorway 10, 13, 15, 18
dovecot 27
drawbridge 4, 14–15, 26, 28–29
Drum Castle, Scotland 21

F
feasts 16
flags 4, 9, 10, 28, 29

G
gatehouse 10–11, 12, 13, 14, 15
great hall 16–17, 18

H
horses 22, 23, 27, 29

I
invaders 12
Irvine, Alexander 21

J
jousting 4, 22, 29

K
kings 4, 7
knights 4, 7, 9, 17, 22, 23, 27, 29

L
lance 22, 23, 29

M
mangonel 4, 24–25, 28
moat 4, 14, 26–27, 28–29

P
portcullis 4, 12–13, 15, 28–29

Q
queens 4, 7

T
tilt yard 4, 22–23, 29
toilets 18, 19
towers 8–9, 11, 13, 14, 15, 28, 29
turrets 4, 8–9, 10, 28, 29

W
windows 8